Y0-AEC-698

KNOW YOUR GOVERNMENT

The Department of Transportation

KNOW YOUR GOVERNMENT

The Department of Transportation

Wallace Charles Stefany

CHELSEA HOUSE PUBLISHERS

ST. PHILIP'S COLLEGE LIBRARY

Editor-in-Chief: Nancy Toff
Executive Editor: Remmel T. Nunn
Managing Editor: Karyn Gullen Browne
Copy Chief: Juliann Barbato
Picture Editor: Adrian G. Allen
Art Director: Giannella Garrett
Manufacturing Manager: Gerald Levine

Staff for THE DEPARTMENT OF TRANSPORTATION

Senior Editor: Elizabeth L. Mauro
Associate Editor: Pierre Hauser
Assistant Editor: Michele A. Merens
Copyeditor: James Guiry
Editorial Assistant: Tara P. Deal
Picture Researcher: Patrick McCaffrey
Designer: Noreen M. Lamb
Production Coordinator: Joseph Romano

Creative Director: Harold Steinberg

Copyright © 1988 by Chelsea House Publishers, a division of Main Line Book Co. All rights reserved. Printed and bound in the United States of America.

First Printing

1 3 5 7 9 8 6 4 2

Library of Congress Cataloging in Publication Data

Stefany, Wallace Charles.
  The Department of Transportation.
  (Know your government)
  Bibliography: p.
  Includes index.
  Summary: Surveys the history of the Department of Transportation and describes its structure, current functions, and influence on American society.
  1. United States. Dept. of Transportation. [1. United States. Dept. of Transportation] I. Title. II. Series: Know your government (New York, N.Y.)
HE206.3.S73   1988   353.86   87-24924
ISBN 0-87754-847-1

CONTENTS

Introduction 7
1 Moving the Nation 15
2 The Growth of Transportation 19
3 The Web of Union 39
4 The New DOT 47
    Feature A Tale of Two Railroads: Amtrak and Conrail 60
5 Inside the DOT 63
6 Regulating Transportation 71
    Feature Public Transportation for the Handicapped 77
7 Transportation and the Future 83
The Department of Transportation Organization 88
Glossary 89
Selected References 91
Index 92

KNOW YOUR GOVERNMENT

- The American Red Cross
- The Bureau of Indian Affairs
- The Central Intelligence Agency
- The Commission on Civil Rights
- The Department of Agriculture
- The Department of the Air Force
- The Department of the Army
- The Department of Commerce
- The Department of Defense
- The Department of Education
- The Department of Energy
- The Department of Health and Human Services
- The Department of Housing and Urban Development
- The Department of the Interior
- The Department of Justice
- The Department of Labor
- The Department of the Navy
- The Department of State
- The Department of Transportation
- The Department of the Treasury
- The Drug Enforcement Administration
- The Environmental Protection Agency
- The Equal Employment Opportunities Commission
- The Federal Aviation Administration
- The Federal Bureau of Investigation
- The Federal Communications Commission
- The Federal Government: How It Works
- The Federal Reserve System
- The Federal Trade Commission
- The Food and Drug Administration
- The Forest Service
- The House of Representatives
- The Immigration and Naturalization Service
- The Internal Revenue Service
- The Library of Congress
- The National Aeronautics and Space Administration
- The National Archives and Records Administration
- The National Foundation on the Arts and Humanities
- The National Park Service
- The National Science Foundation
- The Nuclear Regulatory Commission
- The Peace Corps
- The Presidency
- The Public Health Service
- The Securities and Exchange Commission
- The Senate
- The Small Business Administration
- The Smithsonian
- The Supreme Court
- The Tennessee Valley Authority
- The U.S. Arms Control and Disarmament Agency
- The U.S. Coast Guard
- The U.S. Constitution
- The U.S. Fish and Wildlife Service
- The U.S. Information Agency
- The U.S. Marine Corps
- The U.S. Mint
- The U.S. Postal Service
- The U.S. Secret Service
- The Veterans Administration

CHELSEA HOUSE PUBLISHERS

INTRODUCTION

Government: Crises of Confidence

Arthur M. Schlesinger, jr.

From the start, Americans have regarded their government with a mixture of reliance and mistrust. The men who founded the republic did not doubt the indispensability of government. "If men were angels," observed the 51st Federalist Paper, "no government would be necessary." But men are not angels. Because human beings are subject to wicked as well as to noble impulses, government was deemed essential to assure freedom and order.

At the same time, the American revolutionaries knew that government could also become a source of injury and oppression. The men who gathered in Philadelphia in 1787 to write the Constitution therefore had two purposes in mind. They wanted to establish a strong central authority and to limit that central authority's capacity to abuse its power.

To prevent the abuse of power, the Founding Fathers wrote two basic principles into the new Constitution. The principle of federalism divided power between the state governments and the central authority. The principle of the separation of powers subdivided the central authority itself into three branches—the executive, the legislative, and the judiciary—so that "each may be a check on the other." The *Know Your Government* series focuses on the major executive departments and agencies in these branches of the federal government.

The Constitution did not plan the executive branch in any detail. After vesting the executive power in the president, it assumed the existence of "executive departments" without specifying what these departments should be. Congress began defining their functions in 1789 by creating the Departments of State, Treasury, and War. The secretaries in charge of these departments made up President Washington's first cabinet. Congress also provided for a legal officer, and President Washington soon invited the attorney general, as he was called, to attend cabinet meetings. As need required, Congress created more executive departments.

Setting up the cabinet was only the first step in organizing the American state. With almost no guidance from the Constitution, President Washington, seconded by Alexander Hamilton, his brilliant secretary of the treasury, equipped the infant republic with a working administrative structure. The Federalists believed in both executive energy and executive accountability and set high standards for public appointments. The Jeffersonian opposition had less faith in strong government and preferred local government to the central authority. But when Jefferson himself became president in 1801, although he set out to change the direction of policy, he found no reason to alter the framework the Federalists had erected.

By 1801 there were about 3,000 federal civilian employees in a nation of a little more than 5 million people. Growth in territory and population steadily enlarged national responsibilities. Thirty years later, when Jackson was president, there were more than 11,000 government workers in a nation of 13 million. The federal establishment was increasing at a faster rate than the population.

Jackson's presidency brought significant changes in the federal service. He believed that the executive branch contained too many officials who saw their jobs as "species of property" and as "a means of promoting individual interest." Against the idea of a permanent service based on life tenure, Jackson argued for the periodic redistribution of federal offices, contending that this was the democratic way and that official duties could be made "so plain and simple that men of intelligence may readily qualify themselves for their performance." He called this policy rotation-in-office. His opponents called it the spoils system.

In fact, partisan legend exaggerated the extent of Jackson's removals. More than 80 percent of federal officeholders retained their jobs. Jackson discharged no larger a proportion of government workers than Jefferson had done a generation earlier. But the rise in these years of mass political parties gave federal patronage new importance as a means of building the party and of rewarding activists. Jackson's successors were less restrained in the distribution of spoils. As the federal establishment grew—to nearly 40,000 by 1861—the politicization of the public service excited increasing concern.

After the Civil War the spoils system became a major political issue. High-minded men condemned it as the root of all political evil. The spoilsmen, said the British commentator James Bryce, "have distorted and depraved the mechanism of politics." Patronage, by giving jobs to unqualified, incompetent, and dishonest persons, lowered the standards of public service and nourished corrupt political machines. Office-seekers pursued presidents and cabinet secretaries without mercy. "Patronage," said Ulysses S. Grant after his presidency, "is the bane of the presidential office." "Every time I appoint someone to office," said another political leader, "I make a hundred enemies and one ingrate." George William Curtis, the president of the National Civil Service Reform League, summed up the indictment. He said,

> The theory which perverts public trusts into party spoils, making public employment dependent upon personal favor and not on proved merit, necessarily ruins the self-respect of public employees, destroys the function of party in a republic, prostitutes elections into a desperate strife for personal profit, and degrades the national character by lowering the moral tone and standard of the country.

The object of civil service reform was to promote efficiency and honesty in the public service and to bring about the ethical regeneration of public life. Over bitter opposition from politicians, the reformers in 1883 passed the Pendleton Act, establishing a bipartisan Civil Service Commission, competitive examinations, and appointment on merit. The Pendleton Act also gave the president authority to extend by executive order the number of "classified" jobs—that is, jobs subject to the merit system. The act applied initially only to about 14,000 of the more than 100,000 federal positions. But by the end of the 19th century 40 percent of federal jobs had moved into the classified category.

Civil service reform was in part a response to the growing complexity of American life. As society grew more organized and problems more technical, official duties were no longer so plain and simple that any person of intelligence could perform them. In public service, as in other areas, the all-round man was yielding ground to the expert, the amateur to the professional. The excesses of the spoils system thus provoked the counter-ideal of scientific public administration, separate from politics and, as far as possible, insulated against it.

The cult of the expert, however, had its own excesses. The idea that administration could be divorced from policy was an illusion. And in the realm of policy, the expert, however much segregated from partisan politics, can never attain perfect objectivity. He remains the prisoner of his own set of values. It is these values rather than technical expertise that determine fundamental judgments of public policy. To turn over such judgments to experts, moreover, would be to abandon democracy itself; for in a democracy final decisions must be made by the people and their elected representatives. "The business of the expert," the British political scientist Harold Laski rightly said, "is to be on tap and not on top."

Politics, however, were deeply ingrained in American folkways. This meant intermittent tension between the presidential government, elected every four years by the people, and the permanent government, which saw presidents come and go while it went on forever. Sometimes the permanent government knew better than its political masters; sometimes it opposed or sabotaged valuable new initiatives. In the end a strong president with effective cabinet secretaries could make the permanent government responsive to presidential purpose, but it was often an exasperating struggle.

The struggle within the executive branch was less important, however, than the growing impatience with bureaucracy in society as a whole. The 20th century saw a considerable expansion of the federal establishment. The Great Depression and the New Deal led the national government to take on a variety of new responsibilities. The New Deal extended the federal regulatory apparatus. By 1940, in a nation of 130 million people, the number of federal workers for the first time passed the 1 million mark. The Second World War brought federal civilian employment to 3.8 million in 1945. With peace, the federal establishment declined to around 2 million by 1950. Then growth resumed, reaching 2.8 million by the 1980s.

The New Deal years saw rising criticism of "big government" and "bureaucracy." Businessmen resented federal regulation. Conservatives worried about the impact of paternalistic government on individual self-reliance, on community responsibility, and on economic and personal freedom. The nation in effect renewed the old debate between Hamilton and Jefferson in the early republic, although with an ironic exchange of positions. For the Hamiltonian constituency, the "rich and well-born," once the advocate of affirmative government, now condemned government intervention, while the Jeffersonian constituency, the plain people, once the advocate of a weak central government and of states' rights, now favored government intervention.

In the 1980s, with the presidency of Ronald Reagan, the debate has burst out with unusual intensity. According to conservatives, government intervention abridges liberty, stifles enterprise, and is inefficient, wasteful, and arbitrary. It disturbs the harmony of the self-adjusting market and creates worse troubles than it solves. Get government off our backs, according to the popular cliché, and our problems will solve themselves. When government is necessary, let it be at the local level, close to the people. Above all, stop the inexorable growth of the federal government.

In fact, for all the talk about the "swollen" and "bloated" bureaucracy, the federal establishment has not been growing as inexorably as many Americans seem to believe. In 1949, it consisted of 2.1 million people. Thirty years later, while the country had grown by 70 million, the federal force had grown only by 750,000. Federal workers were a smaller percentage of the population in 1985 than they were in 1955—or in 1940. The federal establishment, in short, has not kept pace with population growth. Moreover, national defense and the postal service account for 60 percent of federal employment.

Why then the widespread idea about the remorseless growth of government? It is partly because in the 1960s the national government assumed new and intrusive functions: affirmative action in civil rights, environmental protection, safety and health in the workplace, community organization, legal aid to the poor. Although this enlargement of the federal regulatory role was accompanied by marked growth in the size of government on all levels, the expansion has taken place primarily in state and local government. Whereas the federal force increased by only 27 percent in the 30 years after 1950, the state and local government force increased by an astonishing 212 percent.

Despite the statistics, the conviction flourishes in some minds that the national government is a steadily growing behemoth swallowing up the liberties of the people. The foes of Washington prefer local government, feeling it is closer to the people and therefore allegedly more responsive to popular needs. Obviously there is a great deal to be said for settling local questions locally. But local government is characteristically the government of the locally powerful. Historically, the way the locally powerless have won their human and constitutional rights has often been through appeal to the national government. The national government has vindicated racial justice against local bigotry, defended the Bill of Rights against local vigilantism, and protected natural resources against local greed. It has civilized industry and secured the rights of labor organizations. Had the states' rights creed prevailed, there would perhaps still be slavery in the United States.

The national authority, far from diminishing the individual, has given most Americans more personal dignity and liberty than ever before. The individual freedoms destroyed by the increase in national authority have been in the main the freedom to deny black Americans their rights as citizens; the freedom to put small children to work in mills and immigrants in sweatshops; the freedom to pay starvation wages, require barbarous working hours, and permit squalid working conditions; the freedom to deceive in the sale of goods and securities; the freedom to pollute the environment—all freedoms that, one supposes, a civilized nation can readily do without.

"Statements are made," said President John F. Kennedy in 1963, "labelling the Federal Government an outsider, an intruder, an adversary. . . . The United States Government is not a stranger or not an enemy. It is the people of fifty states joining in a national effort. . . . Only a great national effort by a great people working together can explore the mysteries of space, harvest the products at the bottom of the ocean, and mobilize the human, natural, and material resources of our lands."

So an old debate continues. However, Americans are of two minds. When pollsters ask large, spacious questions—Do you think government has become too involved in your lives? Do you think government should stop regulating business?—a sizable majority opposes big government. But when asked specific questions about the practical work of government—Do you favor social security? unemployment compensation? Medicare? health and safety standards in factories? environmental protection? government guarantee of jobs for everyone seeking employment? price and wage controls when inflation threatens?—a sizable majority approves of intervention.

In general, Americans do not want less government. What they want is more efficient government. They want government to do a better job. For a time in the 1970s, with Vietnam and Watergate, Americans lost confidence in the national government. In 1964, more than three-quarters of those polled had thought the national government could be trusted to do right most of the time. By 1980 only one-quarter was prepared to offer such trust. But by 1984 trust in the federal government to manage national affairs had climbed back to 45 percent.

Bureaucracy is a term of abuse. But it is impossible to run any large organization, whether public or private, without a bureaucracy's division of labor and hierarchy of authority. And we live in a world of large organizations. Without bureaucracy modern society would collapse. The problem is not to abolish bureaucracy, but to make it flexible, efficient, and capable of innovation.

Two hundred years after the drafting of the Constitution, Americans still regard government with a mixture of reliance and mistrust—a good combination. Mistrust is the best way to keep government reliable. Informed criticism is the means of correcting governmental inefficiency, incompetence, and arbitrariness; that is, of best enabling government to play its essential role. For without government, we cannot attain the goals of the Founding Fathers. Without an understanding of government, we cannot have the informed criticism that makes government do the job right. It is the duty of every American citizen to know our government—which is what this series is all about.

A southern California highway under construction in 1954. An intricate network of highways helps to meet the nation's growing need for efficient transportation routes.

ONE

Moving the Nation

Since colonial days, efficient transportation has been essential to America's social development and economic well-being. In many ways transportation has shaped the nation's growth. The first American cities were located where people and businesses had easy access to shipping ports. Many inland towns were originally rest stops for long-distance travelers.

The colonists used dirt roads and narrow trails to travel from town to town. Over the years, those roads and trails evolved into an intricate network of highways that now services the needs of a nation on the move. Highways, railroads, waterways, and air routes combine to provide Americans with one of the most sophisticated transportation systems in the world. Without the use of these routes, businesses and individuals could not acquire vital goods and services. Ultimately, the nation's economy depends on its transportation.

Because efficient transportation is so vital to the nation, in 1966 the federal government established a cabinet-level department to address the American people's transportation needs. Since then, the Department of Transportation (DOT) has grown to become one of the largest agencies within the executive branch of the federal government. In 1987 the DOT boasted nearly 98,000 employees and a budget of more than $21 billion.

The DOT oversees and coordinates the efforts of nine operating agencies:

A DOT advertising campaign warns against the dangers of drunk driving. The department employs communications specialists to heighten public awareness of transportation safety concerns.

the U.S. Coast Guard, the Federal Aviation Administration, the Federal Highway Administration, the Federal Railroad Administration, the Maritime Administration, the Urban Mass Transportation Administration, the National Highway Traffic Safety Administration, the Saint Lawrence Seaway Development Corporation, and the Research and Special Programs Administration. Supervised by the DOT, these agencies work cooperatively to create and implement hundreds of programs and policies that encourage safe, efficient, and economical transportation throughout the United States.

To promote land transportation, for example, the Federal Highway Administration funds federal highway construction projects. The National Highway Traffic Safety Administration sets safety and fuel economy standards for car manufacturers. The Urban Mass Transportation Administration provides funding to state and local public transportation systems that use buses, subways, or trolleys. The Federal Railroad Administration aids and regulates the nation's railroads. To regulate air traffic, the Federal Aviation Administration approves or vetoes airline mergers and helps negotiate air transport agreements with foreign countries. To manage the nation's waterways, the Maritime Administration maintains open water routes for commercial ships during winter. The U.S. Coast Guard enforces maritime law, protects the marine environment, and maintains a fleet of rescue vessels. Each DOT agency also participates in media campaigns and public awareness programs that promote transportation safety.

These activities suggest the complexity of the DOT's operations. To coordinate and administer the federal government's transportation programs, the department employs specialists in many fields. It recruits experts in air traffic control, rail safety, highway design, and pipeline planning (the flow of natural gas and liquid petroleum through pipelines is considered a form of transportation). The DOT also employs traffic management experts, physicians, lawyers, economists, accountants, and communications specialists who help teach the public about transportation safety and economy.

Not surprisingly, the DOT has become one of the nation's busiest federal agencies. The department strives to safeguard millions of Americans traveling within the country's borders each day. It attempts to provide them with transportation routes and systems that are efficient, convenient, and economical. And it analyzes technological advances that will improve the quality of future transportation systems.

As part of the DOT, the U.S. Coast Guard enforces maritime law, protects the marine environment, and maintains a fleet of rescue vessels.

Travelers in the early 1900s paid their fees at the Old Toll House on the Cumberland Road in Maryland, the nation's first federally maintained turnpike.

TWO

The Growth of Transportation

When European settlers first arrived in America, crude roadways already existed. For centuries American Indians had traveled by foot or on horseback over dirt trails. Early colonists used and often extended these trails to create America's first road system. But as colonial populations and businesses grew, even the extended Indian trails proved to be insufficient travel routes. The colonists began to construct new roads and widen existing ones to meet their needs for greater mobility. In 1667 they completed the Albany–New York highway, one of the nation's first major roadways, along the banks of the Hudson River. Six years later they completed the Boston Post Road, connecting New York City to Boston.

Colonial leaders recognized the importance of maintaining these and other new roads. Some of the nation's earliest laws required citizens to support road construction by providing labor or paying road taxes. But despite the colonists' efforts, dirt roads fell into disrepair as heavy stagecoaches and wagons began to replace travel by foot and on horseback. These vehicles kicked up dust, got stuck in mud, and gouged ruts in the dirt roads, making travel uncomfortable and inconvenient. To alleviate these problems, inventors experimented with innovative methods for paving the dirt roads. They sought to create surfaces that resisted the effects of erosion. One method was to lay planks or logs side by side over the length of the road. Roads paved in this manner were called corduroy roads because their surface resembled the fabric corduroy. These were soon followed by macadamized roads (named after Scottish inventor Loudon McAdam), which used an even layer of crushed rock bound together and sealed over the travel pathway.

The new types of roads made travel easier, but building them required a great deal of money. States often financed road projects within their borders. Private contractors also built roads and charged fees to travelers who used them. These roads, called turnpikes, were America's first toll roads. One of the earliest turnpikes ran from Philadelphia to Lancaster, Pennsylvania, and was completed in 1794.

The federal government became actively involved in transportation issues in 1806, when Congress authorized construction of the first federally maintained turnpike, the National Pike (also called the Cumberland Road, because it began in Cumberland, Maryland). To fund the project, the government used proceeds from federal land grants—a system whereby the federal government gave

Passengers and the U.S. mail traveled by stagecoach during the early 19th century. Dirt roads fell into disrepair as stagecoaches and wagons replaced travel by foot and on horseback.

states plots of land to sell and then allocated the proceeds to road construction projects. Construction on the National Pike began in 1811 and continued until 1852. By the time the road was completed in Vandalia, Illinois, it had cost the government $6.7 million, an enormous sum for that time.

The money the government spent on the National Pike represented only a portion of the amount it was willing to allocate for road construction projects. The same year that Congress appropriated money for the National Pike, it also approved funding to improve and expand the Natchez Trace from an Indian trail into a military road (a road used to transport troops and supplies). The upgraded Natchez Trace later became an important route for frontiersmen traveling between Mississippi and New Orleans, Louisiana.

Although the nation's roads were steadily improving, land travel remained slow, expensive, and uncomfortable. Traders and businessmen demanded faster and cheaper transportation modes. They happily adopted the steamboat, designed in 1786 by American inventor John Fitch. Unlike conventional vessels that were propelled by wind and water currents, the steamboat was propelled

Strollers in 1896 walk alongside the nation's first macadamized road, constructed in Lancaster, Pennsylvania. An even layer of crushed rock, bound together and sealed, paves this type of road.

by a steam-driven engine and therefore free to move either with or against water currents. By 1817 regular steamboat service ferried passengers and cargo in both directions on the Ohio and Mississippi Rivers.

Although steamboats offered efficiency and reliability, they were sometimes dangerous to operate. Highly pressurized boilers on the boats occasionally exploded, killing or injuring passengers and crew. Conditions improved after 1840, when Congress passed a law establishing safety guidelines for the vessels. Meanwhile, steamboat owners downplayed the possibility of danger and invested large sums of money to make their vessels luxurious and comfortable. Because of the measures taken to make steamboats safe and attractive they continued to gain popularity.

The Canal Era

The steamboat's success might not have been as great without the subsequent development of the canal, an artificial waterway built by digging a deep trench to connect two natural bodies of water. Steamboats used canals to haul cargo and carry passengers directly across areas that would otherwise have to be skirted by roundabout overland routes. Canals provided an efficient alternative to costly, time-consuming land travel, and many state governments eagerly funded their construction.

One of America's most important canals in the early 19th century was the 350-mile-long Erie Canal, which opened in October 1825. Proposed by New York governor DeWitt Clinton, the canal was financed by the state for $7 million. It allowed steamboats to travel from Buffalo, located on Lake Erie, to Albany, located on the Hudson River. By way of the Hudson, boats continued to the port of New York City. Use of the Erie Canal reduced both the cost and the duration of the trip from Buffalo to New York City. Tolls charged to shippers enabled New York to recover the cost of building the canal by 1832.

Following New York's success, other states rushed to adopt this popular transport route. Pennsylvania, for example, built a canal linking Pittsburgh and Philadelphia. The federal government also began to finance canal construction and bought more than $1 million worth of stock in four canal companies. By 1835, more than 4,000 miles of canals existed in the United States.

Financed by the state of New York for $7 million, construction of the Erie Canal was completed in 1825. Tolls charged to shippers using the canal enabled New York to recover construction costs by 1832.

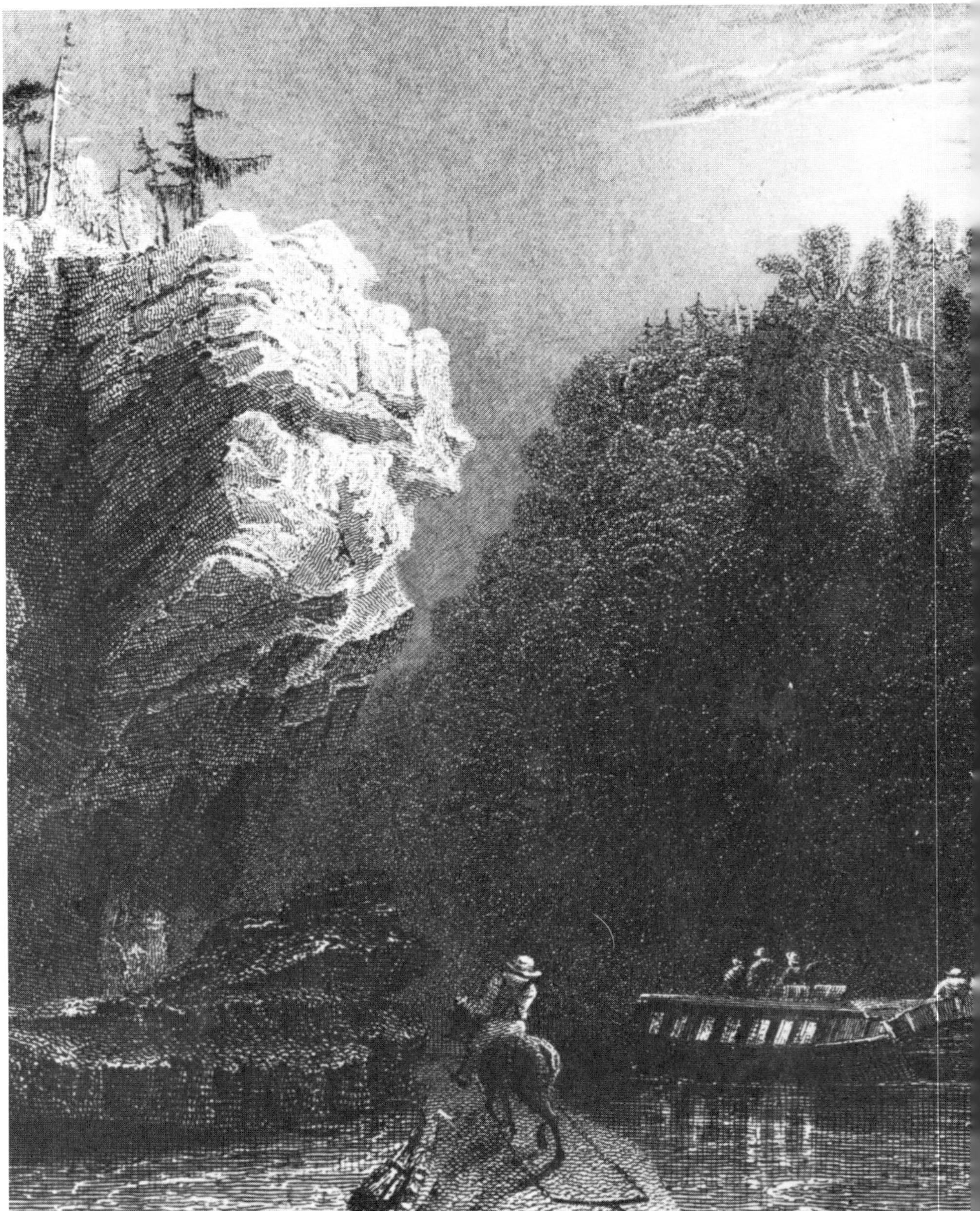

In this 1839 engraving, a steamboat travels on the Erie Canal. The canal enabled steamboats to travel from Buffalo to Albany, New York, where the waterway emptied into the Hudson River.

The William Mason, a Baltimore and Ohio locomotive, was built in 1856. By that time, most Americans had overcome their initial fear of the railroads.

For a time it appeared that canals would become the nation's primary means of transporting people and goods. But by the mid-1800s a new transportation revolution was under way. Steam energy—the power source that fueled the rise of the canals—once again sparked radical change in American travel and shipping.

The Railroad Revolution

In 1804 British engineer Richard Trevithick built the first steam-powered locomotive and promoted it as a vehicle for shipping goods. Twenty years later, British steam engines were pulling as many as 35 cars and carrying loads that weighed as much as 90 tons. Unfortunately, these trains could still go no faster than a horse; a law required that a boy on horseback carry a red flag in front of the engine at all times, to alert people to stay out of the train's way.

Americans soon became intrigued with the "iron horses," as the trains were called. On July 4, 1828, the Baltimore and Ohio Railroad laid the first miles of railroad track in the United States. In the summer of 1830, track work was completed and service began. Shortly thereafter, the Baltimore and Ohio participated in a race in which the first steam engine built in the United States, the Tom Thumb, was pitted against a horse over a few miles of track near Relay, Maryland. Unfortunately, the steam engine broke down over the course of the race. Its owner, American manufacturer Peter Cooper, had failed to prove that a steam engine could outspeed a horse. Nevertheless, the Baltimore and Ohio Railroad recognized the Tom Thumb's potential and put it into service.

On December 25, 1830, a crowd of people in Charleston, South Carolina, witnessed an event that sparked the development of common carriers (trains designed to carry passengers instead of goods). On that day, stockholders in a railroad company held an exhibition in which a steam engine, The Best Friend of Charleston, successfully carried passengers across a few miles of track. The next day, regular passenger service began in Charleston. Other states soon followed suit.

The Fearsome Iron Horse

At first, the railroads were objects of suspicion and dread. Many people were afraid of these machines, which could travel faster than any previous mode of transportation. Some doctors warned that traveling at speeds of more than 20 miles per hour would cause passengers to suffer concussions. Many farmers worried that the loud roar of moving trains would frighten their cows so much that they would stop giving milk.

Politicians and government leaders were concerned that the railroads would cause the booming business associated with the canals to vanish. In 1829 New York governor Martin Van Buren wrote to President Andrew Jackson that he should "protect the American people from the evils of 'railroads' and . . . preserve the canals for posterity." He further warned that trains "are pulled at the enormous speed of 15 miles per hour by 'engines,' which, in addition to endangering life and limb of passengers, roar and snort their way through the countryside, setting fire to the crops, scaring the livestock, and frightening women and children." Van Buren concluded, "The Almighty certainly never intended that people should travel at such breakneck speed."

Despite such opposition, railroads became immensely popular in the 19th century. In much the same way as the federal government had aided road construction, it took an active role in developing the country's railroads with funds obtained through land grants. By 1849 almost 6,000 miles of railroad tracks lined the eastern seaboard. Between 1850 and 1871 the government also provided railroad companies with acres of vacant land and encouraged them to extend their lines to newly established states in western and southern parts of the country. In return for this assistance, the railroads agreed to carry government cargo and passengers at about half the regularly charged rates. These incentives proved to be enormously successful, and by the end of the

Workers lay the track for the Pacific Railroad. By the 1870s, railroads had revolutionized passenger travel and replaced canals as the most efficient mode of commercial transportation.

1880s more than 150,000 miles of railroad tracks crisscrossed the United States.

Although many fears that people expressed about the railroads were unfounded, at least one concern proved to be prophetic: The canal era had ended. The railroads claimed several advantages over canals. They could be

The growth of the railroads during the 1870s threatened to encroach on the nation's farmland. In this 1873 political cartoon, a farmer tries to fend off the "railroad monster."

built over any kind of terrain, whereas canals could be built only where land was relatively low and level. In addition, railroad tracks could be constructed anywhere, whereas canals had to be built near lakes or rivers. Finally, people and goods could travel faster and less expensively by railroad than by canal boat.

Some states tried to save their canals by not allowing railroads to accept certain freight contracts. Other states charged tolls to trains carrying goods that previously had been transported by canal boats. Nevertheless, the speed and efficiency of trains ultimately made them the transportation method of choice. By the 1880s canals, which just 50 years earlier had dominated American transportation, had become nearly obsolete.

Federal Regulation Begins

Although the railroads revolutionized passenger travel, they made their greatest impact on American commerce. Trains made it possible to transport goods across the country in mere days instead of weeks. As a result, many businesses began to ship their products by train, and the railroad companies profited.

Despite these gains, certain railroad companies sought to obtain even greater profits by engaging in unfair practices. Railroads often granted low rates, rebates, and other favors to businesses that shipped large quantities of goods; at the same time, they denied space to small businesses. Some firms also charged exorbitant rates in areas inaccessible to other transportation systems. Furthermore, large railroad companies often conspired to fix prices

The Wright Brothers' Kitty Hawk flyer made its first successful flight in 1903 and ushered in the age of air travel.

Cars line Pennsylvania Avenue in Washington, D.C. Widespread automobile use during the 1920s forced the federal government and state governments to construct or improve paved roads.

at rates lower than the smaller companies could afford to match, thereby forcing them out of business.

In response to these abuses, a railroad-reform movement developed in the 1870s and gained momentum in the 1880s. In 1887 Congress passed the Interstate Commerce Act to prohibit railroads from discriminating against small companies on interstate hauls. The act created the Interstate Commerce Commission (ICC) to regulate the rates and services of interstate carrier lines. The ICC represented the government's first attempt to provide Americans with fair access to transportation. Several laws passed in the early 1900s increased the ICC's authority. By 1906 the ICC was setting maximum rail rates that prevented railroads from charging shippers unreasonable fares.

Meanwhile, transportation modes continued to improve as the United States entered the 20th century. Experiments with internal combustion engines produced machines that could move in previously unimagined ways. In 1903 the Wright Brothers' Kitty Hawk flyer made its first successful flight. And in the same decade, a new mode of private transportation—a horseless carriage propelled by an internal combustion engine—attracted enormous attention among inventors and entrepreneurs.

America on Wheels

In 1908 industrialist Henry Ford introduced a product that forever changed the American life-style—the Model T. Ford billed his product as the first affordable motorcar for the general public and sold thousands of them over the next few years. Other companies soon began to manufacture and sell automobiles for both private and commercial use. By 1915 cars could be found in most of America's largest cities and smallest towns. The automotive age had begun.

The widespread use of automobiles forced the federal government to confront a persistent fault in the American transportation system—the lack of paved roads. During the growth of the railroad industry in the 1800s, many roads had fallen into disrepair. To remedy this situation, Congress passed the Federal Aid Road Act, or Tice Law, in 1916. Under this act, the federal

In 1908, Henry Ford introduced the Model T. By 1915, Americans across the nation were buying and driving cars from several automobile manufacturers.

government could help improve or construct state roads by matching state road funds. In return for this assistance, states agreed to work with one another to create an interstate highway system. Between 1920 and 1940 federal funds helped pay for the construction of 1,384,000 miles of paved roads.

The Birth of the Airline Industry

The airline industry also took flight during the first half of the 20th century. In 1918 the federal Post Office Department inaugurated airmail service, using Army Signal Corps pilots and planes to fly the mail between New York, Philadelphia, and Washington, D.C. By 1921 the Post Office Department had added a transcontinental route linking New York and San Francisco with a series of four shorter routes. Four years later, Congress passed a law encouraging commercial airlines to contract for airmail delivery, and by 1927 the entire transcontinental route was under contract.

Meanwhile, the public was becoming intrigued by airplanes. The first commercial airline for passengers started operations in 1926, but many Americans still viewed air travel as a dangerous novelty rather than a practical option. Charles Lindbergh's solo flight across the Atlantic Ocean one year later fired the public's enthusiasm for air travel. And technological advances, such as the development of two-way radio communication from ground to air, made air travel safer. But airplane instruments were still faulty, air traffic control techniques were primitive, and accidents were common.

Until the late 1930s, the airline industry consisted of a handful of private companies building and flying planes without a standardized system of regulations or air traffic routes. The Civil Aeronautics Act of 1938 helped stabilize the airline industry by consolidating federal authority for aviation. The act created the Civil Aeronautics Authority to regulate commercial airlines and the Air Safety Board to investigate airplane accidents. Congress appropriated more than $14 million to improve airplane safety and construction.

Regulations Abound

As federal funding for transportation increased, however, so did federal regulations. During the first half of the 20th century, greater mobility in the population gradually increased the government's involvement with all aspects of national transportation. Congress gave the ICC authority to regulate motor

A 1936 Pan American Airways "Clipper" plane flies over the Pacific Ocean. Technological advances and stricter federal regulations made air travel more attractive to passengers by the late 1930s.

Herbert Hoover speaks before a 1947 House committee meeting. Hoover's panel of government experts recommended transferring all federal transportation functions to the Department of Commerce.

vehicles in 1935 and ships in 1940. Also in 1940, Congress approved the creation of the Civil Aeronautics Board (CAB), encompassing the Civil Aeronautics Authority and the Air Safety Board, and authorized it to regulate the airline industry. In 1944 Congress legislated massive highway improvements throughout the nation, setting new standards for highway construction.

By 1945 the government had established regulations for the country's railroads, automobiles, ships, and airplanes. But the government's system of regulating each mode of transportation separately caused numerous problems. Different government agencies and divisions were authorized to issue regulations, and the guidelines they developed were often contradictory or redundant. The country lacked a government agency that could coordinate transportation information and laws.

Many legislators began to favor a comprehensive approach to transportation. In 1947 Senator Homer Capehart of Indiana and Representative Karl Stefan of Nebraska introduced a bill calling for a single, cabinet-level department to coordinate federal transportation activities and administer regulations. They charged that the federal government had dealt inadequately with issues relating to transportation.

The bill faced political opposition and died without coming to a final vote. But it prompted others to consider merging the separate federal agencies dealing with transportation. Later that year, the Commission on Organization of the Executive Branch of Government—a government panel headed by former president Herbert Hoover—issued the first of two reports that recommended transferring all federal transportation functions to the Department of Commerce. Once again, however, opponents quashed the proposal. The nation rode into the 1950s without a unified transportation department.

Indiana senator Homer Capehart poses behind a mountain of legislative paperwork. In 1947, Capehart introduced a bill calling for a cabinet-level agency to coordinate federal transportation activities and regulations.

In this 1948 photograph, drums of vegetable oil are hoisted from railway floats onto a cargo ship. Railroad industry setbacks during the 1940s affected companies that relied on them to ship their goods.

THREE

The Web of Union

In the years following World War II, Americans entered an era of prosperity and consumerism, spending more of their earnings to buy consumer goods than ever before. By the mid-1950s, 75 percent of America's families owned at least one automobile, and car manufacturers continued to profit from sales of their newest luxury models. Trucking companies shipped goods to all parts of the country and enjoyed a healthy surge in business. And buses and taxis coped with crowds in the business districts of most cities and towns. The nation's roadways were strained to accommodate increasing numbers of motor vehicles, even as state and federally supported construction projects continued to build thousands of miles of new roads.

Meanwhile, commercial air travel had become a booming business. Soon after the war, jet-propelled aircraft began to replace piston-engine planes and cut air travel time in half. Suddenly, a coast-to-coast plane trip took only five hours. Millions of travelers discovered they could quickly and safely reach their destinations in airplanes. Jet aircraft also changed the way many American companies conducted business; faster transit was more productive, so manufacturers began to ship more cargo by plane.

Increased automobile and airplane travel seriously affected the nation's older transportation systems, particularly the railroads. Many people who had

A desert highway under construction in California in 1947. After World War II, state and federally supported construction projects added thousands of miles of new roads to the nation's highway network.

previously relied on trains now opted to travel by car or plane. As a result, railroad profits declined, and the nation's railroads began to deteriorate, as some companies deferred plans to upgrade tracks and equipment.

Setbacks in the railroad industry had a serious impact on companies that relied on more than one mode of transportation to ship their goods. For example, farmers, mining companies, and some manufacturers routinely shipped their goods by train to a distribution point and from there, by truck to retail outlets. For this vital segment of the American business community, railroads were an invaluable transportion link.

The interplay between different transportation methods pointed out problems in existing regulations. Each transportation system was regulated individually, and companies that used more than one method to ship their products had to file numerous forms and requests with several government agencies before their goods could leave the factories. Companies complained that the agencies were poorly organized and ineffective.

Meanwhile, the public was becoming concerned that existing federal regulations did not adequately address transportation safety. In the early 1960s lawyer and consumer advocate Ralph Nader attacked the auto industry for its inadequate safety standards. Nader's book, *Unsafe at Any Speed*, focused public attention on design and manufacturing flaws that made certain cars hazardous to drive. Numerous consumer groups were formed in response to Nader's revelations about unsafe automobiles. These groups pressured the government to reexamine transportation safety standards.

By the mid-1960s, government leaders could no longer ignore public pleas for transportation reform. In 1966 President Lyndon Johnson sent a proposal to Congress outlining plans for a federal transportation department. He noted that "In a nation that spans a continent, transportation is the web of union." And yet, he pointed out, U.S. transportation regulations were inefficient and ineffective:

> We spend billions for constructing new highways, but comparatively little for traffic control devices. We spend millions for fast jet aircraft—but little on the traveler's problem of getting to and from the airport. We have mounted a sizable government highway program to expand exports, yet we allow a mountain of red-tape paperwork to negate our efforts. Worldwide, a total of 810 forms are required to cover all types of cargo imported and exported. In this country alone, as many as 43 separate forms are used in one export shipment. . . . This is paperwork run wild.

After World War II, automobile manufacturers produced luxury cars for Americans eager to buy consumer goods; here, a woman poses in her 1947 Studebaker.

Johnson recommended creating a single department to oversee and coordinate the efforts of all federal agencies involved in transportation improvement and safety. The department that he recommended would encompass the Office of the Under Secretary of Commerce for Transportation, the Bureau of Public Roads, the Federal Aviation Agency, the U.S. Coast Guard, the Maritime Administration, the Great Lakes Pilotage Administration, the Saint Lawrence Seaway Development Corporation, and the Alaska Railroad. (Regulatory functions would remain with such independent agencies as the ICC and the CAB.)

In addition, Johnson proposed establishing a national transportation safety board to assume safety and inspection functions previously administered by the ICC and the CAB. The proposed board would review accidents to determine their causes and assess the adequacy of existing safety standards. He also recommended that the federal government create a national highway research and test facility and undertake a six-year, $700-million program to promote state highway and automotive safety. The president urged Congress to

Consumer advocate Ralph Nader poses on an overpass in Washington, D.C., in 1970. His attack on the auto industry's inadequate safety standards in the 1960s led to the formation of numerous consumer groups.

A truck crushes a fragile Volkswagen in a demonstration held during the 1960s. Concerned by the results of such demonstrations, consumer groups pressured the government to reexamine safety standards for automobile manufacturers.

legislate safety standards for motor vehicle tires sold or shipped in the United States. And he sought to ensure safety on national waterways by calling for more stringent federal regulation of seafaring lines.

Congress responded to these proposals by introducing transportation bills in both the House and the Senate. Both bills passed, and after ironing out the differences between the two, Congress passed Public Law 89-670 establishing the Transportation Department.

The act created a department with five operating divisions: the U.S. Coast Guard, transferred from the Treasury Department; the Federal Aviation Administration, formerly an independent agency; the Federal Highway Administration, which included the Bureau of Public Roads, the National Highway Safety Bureau, and the Bureau of Motor Carrier Safety; the Federal Railroad Administration, which included the Bureau of Railroad Safety, the Alaska Railroad, and the Office of High-Speed Ground Transportation; and the Saint Lawrence Seaway Development Corporation, transferred from the Commerce

President Lyndon B. Johnson signs the 1966 bill that created the Department of Transportation.

Department. The act also created the National Transportation Safety Board (NTSB) to investigate and determine the cause of aircraft, railway, highway, and pipeline accidents, and to draft recommendations on transportation safety. (The NTSB became an independent agency in 1975.)

President Johnson was dismayed when he learned that Congress had not incorporated all of his recommendations into the DOT. For example, powerful labor and lobbyist opposition prevented the Maritime Administration from being placed under the department's authority. Nevertheless, Johnson signed the bill into law on October 15, 1966, and enthusiastically applauded the creation of the department as a "major step in bringing our government up to date with the times."

Lady Bird Johnson, shown here planting a tree in a Texas state park, supported the passage of the Highway Beautification Act as part of her national beautification project.

FOUR

The New DOT

In April 1967 the newly created DOT began operations. President Johnson chose Alan S. Boyd to assume the DOT's highest supervisory post, secretary of transportation. Boyd had previously served as chairman of the Civil Aeronautics Board and under secretary of commerce for transportation.

Under Boyd's supervision, the department concentrated on improving transportation safety. Two pieces of legislation aided in this effort. The National Traffic and Motor Vehicle Safety Act enabled the DOT to investigate suspected defects in motor vehicles and order manufacturer recalls when necessary. It also allowed the DOT to set safety standards for brakes, safety belts, energy-absorbing steering columns, and crash padding. The Highway Safety Act allowed the DOT to work with states, local communities, interested organizations and individuals, and the National Highway Safety Advisory Committee to create national highway safety programs. These programs included periodic reexamination of drivers and vehicles, as well as improvements in traffic control devices.

During the DOT's first year of operation, its agencies helped promote the department's commitment to safety. For example, the U.S. Coast Guard assisted more than 3,000 vessels and aircraft, saved 3,028 lives, inspected 30,100 vessels, approved plans for approximately 34,000 vessels, and conducted more than 4,800 investigations of serious or fatal accidents. The Federal Aviation Administration installed advanced equipment and instituted new procedures at New York City regional airports to relieve air traffic congestion. The Federal Railroad Administration processed numerous rail safety cases that had been transferred from the ICC. It also reviewed railroad safety problems and enforcement activities.

Environmental issues also shaped the goals of Boyd's administration. The law that created the DOT required it to consider environmental factors when deciding where to locate federally funded highways. Secretary Boyd emphasized this issue's importance by noting that highways or freeways should be "an integral part of the community, not a cement barrier or concrete river which threatens to inundate an urban area."

In 1967 the department announced its plan to develop an urban transportation

Alan S. Boyd became the first secretary of transportation in 1967. Under his supervision, the department's major goals were to increase transportation safety and to design highways that would complement the surrounding environment.

John A. Volpe became secretary of transportation in 1969. During his term, Congress authorized the DOT to promote and subsidize urban mass transportation, rail passenger service, and rail safety.

program that would consider the impact of city highways on urban environments. The new program authorized using federal highway funds to create design-concept teams of traffic engineers, city planners, and other experts. Their tasks were to design city highways that would complement the surrounding environment and to help solve problems that delayed construction of urban segments of interstate highways.

Meanwhile, the Federal Highway Administration helped the department fulfill its commitment to the environment by administering the Highway Beautification Act. Under this act, more than 1,000 roadside junkyards were removed, and more than 6,000 highway landscaping projects were developed during 1967.

In its second year, the department added a sixth operating division, the Urban Mass Transportation Administration. This new division was formed to help local governments design and maintain public transportation vehicles and facilities. It determined safety standards and procedures for bus, trolley, and subway systems across the nation.

A Change of Leadership

When Richard Nixon succeeded Johnson as president in 1969, he chose John A. Volpe, a former governor of Massachusetts, to replace Boyd as secretary of transportation. Volpe's background in transportation included service as a federal highway administrator during the 1950s.

Volpe reorganized the Office of the Secretary. He merged the offices that had been responsible for developing transportation policy and managing international relations. He also emphasized the importance of environmental affairs by appointing an assistant secretary to direct the department's activities in this area.

During Volpe's term, Congress passed several laws that expanded the department's authority and functions. Congress authorized the department to promote and subsidize urban mass transportation, rail passenger service, and rail safety. It also provided emergency loans to transportation companies experiencing financial difficulties.

Perhaps the most significant legislation during Volpe's tenure was the Rail Passenger Service Act of 1970. This act established the federally supported National Railroad Passenger Corporation, popularly known as Amtrak. During the 1960s, poor financial returns on investments and declines in freight and commuter business had threatened to cripple the railroad industry. Amtrak's goal was to persuade financially troubled railroad companies to pool their

In 1970, the federal government established Amtrak by merging financially troubled passenger railroad companies.

resources and create a truly national rail passenger service.

Congress initially appropriated $40 million to develop Amtrak. The project also received $100 million in federal loan guarantees and $200 million in cash and equipment from 19 railroads participating in the venture. In May 1971 Amtrak began operating a 26,000-mile passenger train network.

Pinpointing the Problems

Volpe's successor, Claude Brinegar, continued to concentrate on efforts that would help the troubled railroad industry. In 1973 Congress passed the Regional Rail Reorganization Act to create the Consolidated Rail Corporation, or Conrail. The purpose of Conrail—created by combining seven bankrupt or failing northeastern rail carriers—was to restructure the northeastern United States' ailing rail freight system and make it profitable again. (The act stipulated that Conrail would return to private ownership when it began to make money.)

In early 1974 the DOT established guidelines for streamlining the rail freight system and eliminating excess trackage. This plan formed the basis of the Railroad Revitalization and Regulatory Reform Act of 1976, which provided financial aid to railroads and urged less rigid regulation. The act also gave Conrail a $2.1 billion loan.

The Restructured Department

During the 1970s the Department of Transportation underwent a number of structural changes. Early in the decade, Secretary Brinegar established the Office of the Assistant Secretary for Congressional and Intergovernmental Affairs. Other structural changes occurred in the late 1970s under Transportation Secretary Brock Adams, appointed by President Jimmy Carter in 1977.

Adams' administration reflected a change in national transportation policy. In 1978 Adams noted that the nation was undergoing a transition from a time of building, developing, and expanding transportation systems to a time of more prudent management of existing systems. He emphasized the need to fully utilize existing systems while studying their effects on environmental quality and their abilities to meet consumers' needs.

Adams's efforts to reduce the personnel and scope of the Office of the Secretary underscored his intention to manage the department more conservatively. He eliminated or consolidated many positions, reducing the number of

Brock Adams became secretary of transportation in 1977. He emphasized the need to use existing transportation systems fully while monitoring their abilities to meet consumers' demands.

employees in the Office of the Secretary by about 970.

To further increase efficiency, Adams created the Research and Special Programs Administration in 1977. Its major divisions—the Materials Transportation Bureau, the Transportation Programs Bureau, and the Transportation Systems Center—administered certain programs that had previously been assigned to the Office of the Secretary. By 1980 the administration had established an automotive research program, initiated regulatory actions involving hazardous materials and pipeline safety, and improved emergency preparedness.

Brock also consolidated the DOT's audit and criminal investigation activities. He established the Office of the Inspector General to investigate fraud or abuse in DOT-related activities and to examine ways to reduce costs and improve efficiency.

Meanwhile, Congress was working to make transportation industries more efficient by reforming many of the department's regulations. Many industry representatives, lobbyists, and government officials supported deregulation, a process whereby existing government controls on the industries would slowly be lifted and then eliminated. They asserted that federal regulations, such as those that controlled the setting of fares, prevented transportation companies from competing for the public's business. They also argued that the government no longer had to exercise the caution it once did in dealing with private industries, because public demand would force companies to perform efficiently and safely. In addition, the federal government would save personnel, time, and money by reducing its regulatory duties.

Congress was receptive to these views and passed legislation to liberalize many of the department's regulations. The Motor Carrier Act of 1980 relaxed requirements for entering the trucking industry. It also set new trucking service rates that were expected to save consumers almost $8 billion annually. Another reform bill, the Staggers Rail Act of 1980, gave the railroads more flexibility to set rates, along with new opportunities to improve service and reduce operating costs.

Meanwhile, regulatory agencies, such as the ICC and the CAB, also came under review. Deregulation proponents claimed that these agencies were discouraging transportation companies from competing with each other by setting uniform maximum rates on travel and cargo hauls. In response to these claims, Congress passed the Airline Deregulation Act of 1978, which lessened the CAB's power to regulate domestic air rates and routes over a six-year period. And in 1980 Congress ordered the ICC to lift many of its route and rate regulations for rail and motor freight (trucking) traffic.

Controversy and the DOT

During the summer of 1981 controversy marred the DOT's efforts to control transportation costs without jeopardizing safety. During salary negotiations, some 13,000 members of the Professional Air Traffic Controllers Organization (PATCO) demanded higher pay and approximately $700 million in benefits. Instead, the union members were offered $40 million in benefits. Negotiations became bogged down, and on August 3, 1981, the air traffic controllers declared a strike.

Because the controllers were officially employed by the FAA, federal law prohibited them from striking. The federal government refused to negotiate with the controllers until the strike was halted, but PATCO wanted an agreement before sending its members back to work. Meanwhile, the FAA

Members of the Professional Air Traffic Controllers Organization (PATCO) on strike in 1981. The government fired the air traffic controllers, who disobeyed a federal law prohibiting them from striking.

recruited supervisors, military personnel, and nonstriking controllers to direct air traffic at airports across the country. It also imposed a 50 percent cutback in flights at 22 major airports. By enforcing these measures, airports were able to keep operating during the standoff and scheduled air service declined to only 75 to 86 percent of normal volume.

President Ronald Reagan had appointed a new DOT secretary, Drew Lewis, in 1981. Lewis took a hard line against the strikers. He warned that there would be "no turning back, no second chance" for strikers who ignored the government's order to return to work. The union chose to ignore Lewis's warning, claiming their extraordinarily stressful job conditions endangered passengers' lives. On August 5, 1981, the government shocked PATCO—and the nation—by firing the strikers.

In October 1981 the Federal Labor Relations Authority revoked PATCO's right to represent its members. Stripped of union dues—the organization's

Travelers whose flights have been canceled crowd New York's Kennedy Airport during the 1981 air traffic controllers' strike. Such scenes were relatively rare, owing to the efforts of officials appointed to stand in for the controllers.

Elizabeth H. Dole succeeded Drew Lewis as secretary of transportation in 1982. Under her administration, the department again focused on improving safety.

only source of income—and faced with enormous fines for violating back-to-work orders, PATCO eventually went bankrupt. The DOT had exerted its authority and won.

A New Secretary

Secretary Lewis resigned from his post in December 1982 to take a job in private industry. His successor, Elizabeth H. Dole, brought a new focus to the secretary's office. Dole had been Reagan's assistant for consumer matters before he named her secretary of transportation. Upon accepting the post, Dole once again emphasized the importance of improving safety in all areas of transportation.

Dole used the news media to educate the public about the value of safe driving habits, such as using seat belts and observing established speed limits. Her administration also used advertising campaigns to heighten the public's

Federally supported Conrail became profitable in 1985 and was put up for sale. Conrail stock was first sold on the New York Stock Exchange in March 1987 and brought $1.6 billion into the federal treasury.

awareness about the dangers of driving under the influence of drugs and alcohol.

The new secretary also continued to oversee programs that the DOT had initiated before her term in office. For example, by the time Dole assumed her duties in 1983, the CAB no longer had the power to regulate domestic air routes and fares; instead it handled details concerning international fares and rates, mergers, and consumer matters. A staff of 850 employees had dwindled to 300. During Dole's term, the DOT took on the task of absorbing the CAB's remaining employees and functions.

Dole's administration also participated in the final round of negotiations on another long-term DOT project. In 1985 Dole announced that federally supported Conrail had become profitable and was therefore eligible for private ownership. The railroad was put up for sale at a price of $1.9 billion. Norfolk Southern Corporation expressed interest in buying Conrail and the Senate approved the sale. Some members of the House of Representatives, however, opposed the purchase. They noted that if Conrail was sold to Norfolk Southern, the line might gain a monopoly (an unfair advantage) over its competitors. This opposition delayed a House vote. By August 1986 Norfolk Southern had tired of waiting and withdrew its offer.

After the Norfolk Southern deal collapsed, Secretary Dole said she would work with Congress "to develop a public offering alternative." In November 1986 she announced that the government would offer its estimated 25 million shares of Conrail stock for public sale in the spring of 1987. Dole predicted that the stock sale, perhaps the largest offering in U.S. history, would provide the government with as much as $1.6 billion. She called Conrail's sale "the flagship example" of President Reagan's commitment to private ownership of transportation systems.

Conrail stock was sold on the New York Stock Exchange in March 1987 and, as anticipated, brought $1.6 billion into the federal treasury. The DOT had successfully developed and delivered a valuable commodity to the American public. Conrail's success proved that the department could offer constructive, and even profitable, solutions to problems affecting the country's transportation networks.

A Tale of Two Railroads: Amtrak and Conrail

During the 1960s, many of the nation's passenger railroads were verging on bankruptcy. Travelers preferred fast airplanes or roomy automobiles on long-distance trips. The freight rail industry was also threatened by stiff competition from the trucking industry.

Realizing that the passenger and freight rail industries were in danger of disappearing altogether, the federal government stepped in to help the railroads. In 1970, Congress created Amtrak, a national passenger rail service, by merging financially troubled regional passenger railroads. And in 1976, Congress created Conrail, by merging seven failing passenger and freight railroads in the country's northeastern industrial region.

Although both of these railroads were federally subsidized and supervised by the Department of Transportation (DOT), they operated with separate business strategies. As a result, Conrail eventually became profitable when its management took advantage of an opportunity: federal deregulation of the freight rail industry, which encouraged competition among freight carriers. Amtrak, however, continued to struggle financially.

Initially, Amtrak used its federal subsidies to renovate the equipment it had inherited from the regional railroads and to attract customers with promises of luxurious train travel. During the early 1970s, this plan seemed to work. Long-distance passenger service increased by 5 percent each year, and large numbers of northeastern commuters began riding Amtrak's rails to and from work. Amtrak developed into a modestly successful railroad whose passengers enjoyed low fares, thanks to federal subsidies. Although Amtrak could not hope to compete against the airline industry, which commanded more than three-fourths of the long-distance travel market, there was a chance it could compete with the bus industry, which commanded a much smaller share of this market.

During its first five years, Conrail also repaired equipment on its northeastern passenger and freight lines, with $7 billion in subsidies. But the company's business strategy changed in 1980, when Congress passed the Staggers Rail Act. This law allowed freight railroads to set their own fares, enabling them to compete with the trucking industry.

Conrail immediately seized this opportunity to become a major shipper. Because the company had been upgrading its equipment since 1976, it was able to offer customers improved freight lines as soon as deregulation went into effect in 1981. And because it was funded by federal subsidies, it could also offer customers low rates. Conrail soon transferred its northeastern passenger lines to state transportation authorities in order to concentrate solely on the freight business. These changes proved successful, and by the end of 1981 Conrail had turned a small profit.

Former Transportation Secretary Elizabeth Dole and President Ronald Reagan hold a symbolic "check" commemorating the sale of Conrail stock, which provided the U.S. government with more than $1 billion.

Amtrak's financial outlook was not as optimistic in the early 1980s. Federal deregulation of the airline industry in 1978 had enabled the airlines to attract even more long-distance travelers with low fares and improved services. Amtrak's national share of long-distance passengers dropped to a mere 2 percent. Its status as a national passenger rail service prevented it from selling rail lines that attracted few passengers, in order to cut costs during this no-growth period. The company continually had to ask the government for large subsidies.

By 1985, the differences between the passenger and freight rail industries—and between Amtrak and Conrail—were marked. Conrail had become a profitable shipping company, while Amtrak was operating at a loss.

According to its congressional charter, Conrail was to be sold when it became profitable. In 1987, the DOT engineered a public offering of Conrail stock, and the government received $1.6 billion from the sale. Also in 1987, President Ronald Reagan asked Congress to consider selling Amtrak's profitable northeastern passenger line, in order to reduce the total amount of the federal funding allocated to the company.

The federal government took a gamble when it tried to help the railroads during the 1970s and 1980s. Many people view the 1987 sale of Conrail as one of the DOT's greatest successes and the continued financial troubles of Amtrak as one of its most embarrassing failures. Surely, helping the railroads has been one of the DOT's toughest challenges.

The DOT headquarters in Washington, D.C., supervises nine operating divisions and six regional offices located around the country.

FIVE

Inside the DOT

In a nation that relies on transportation as heavily as the United States does, the DOT has had to assume a variety of responsibilities. To fulfill them, the department employs more than 95,000 people in its nine divisions and six regional offices. Its employees include engineers, lawyers, researchers, environmentalists, safety experts, administrators, and personnel from many other professions. Most of these people work at the department's headquarters in southwest Washington, D.C. Others are employed at regional offices located in Philadelphia, Atlanta, Chicago, Fort Worth, Kansas City, and San Francisco. In addition, air traffic controllers are employed at airports all over the country.

At the helm of this enormous operation stands the secretary of transportation, appointed by the president to serve as his chief adviser and national spokesperson on transportation issues. The deputy secretary is also appointed by the president. Their office plans, directs, and controls all departmental activities, including policy formation, distribution of resources and functions among departmental agencies and divisions, and program evaluation.

The Office of the Secretary includes many departments that help the secretary perform these functions. Among the most important are the Office of the General Counsel, which oversees the department's legal affairs, and the Office of the Inspector General, which audits the department's budget and

The DOT's Office of Public Affairs works with the news media and produces publications to educate the public about transportation.

investigates fraud in DOT-related activities. The general counsel and the inspector general are appointed to these offices by the president.

Five assistant secretaries' offices are responsible for setting broad objectives and carrying out administrative functions for the DOT's operating divisions. The Office of Policy and International Affairs develops, reviews, and coordinates policy for domestic and international transportation. Among other duties, the office works cooperatively with foreign governments to exchange scientific and technical information pertaining to transportation. It also sets policies on matters related to international trade and processes complaints about unfair practices in international fares, rates, and tariffs. The Office of Budget and Programs coordinates the budget requirements of the various DOT programs and advises the secretary on the financial management of the department. The Office of Governmental Affairs directs the department's legislative programs and coordinates its relationship with Congress, state and local governments, and various special-interest groups. The Office of Administration manages the department's daily affairs, including personnel training, security, and general management. Finally, the Office of Public Affairs directs media relations and distributes transportation information to the public.

Some divisions of the secretary's office serve and protect the public directly. For example, the Office of Civil Rights works to ensure that the DOT and its contractors abide by civil rights and equal opportunity laws when hiring employees. The Minority Business Resource Center encourages minority-owned businesses to participate in DOT-sponsored programs. The Contract Appeals Board hears legal appeals and issues final decisions about department contracts. The Office of Commercial Space Transportation promotes public investment in and operation of unmanned booster rockets that place commercial satellites in orbit.

The DOT's Maritime Administration regulates U.S. commercial shipping. Here, freight is unloaded from a cargo boat docked in the port of Seattle.

The Operating Divisions

The DOT contains nine operating divisions, each of which performs various safety and administrative functions related to a particular mode of transportation or department project. For example, the Federal Railroad Administration develops policies and safety programs relating to the nation's railways. And the Saint Lawrence Seaway Development Corporation manages projects pertaining to the commercial sea-lane that runs in and along the Saint Lawrence River from Montreal, Canada, to Lake Erie. Each division is headed by an administrator who is chosen by and reports to the secretary.

The U.S. Coast Guard, the Maritime Agency, and the Saint Lawrence Seaway Development Corporation address issues relating to the nation's ship traffic and waterways. The Federal Highway Administration and the National Highway Traffic Safety Administration address automotive concerns and road development and maintenance. The Federal Aviation Administration monitors the nation's air traffic, while the Federal Railroad Administration concentrates on issues affecting the country's railroads. The Urban Mass Transportation Administration addresses issues concerning subways, trolleys, buses, and other aspects of urban public transportation. The Research and Special Programs Administration is charged with gathering research and designing programs that will help the other transportation agencies implement their specific programs or policies.

The DOT acts as an umbrella organization, supervising the activities of these agencies and carrying their proposals to the president and Congress for consideration. However, the units themselves are responsible for developing the specific plans and programs that carry out policy.

Working with Congress

The DOT has a complex relationship with Congress, which monitors the department's activities. The Senate must approve high-level DOT appointees, such as the secretary, the deputy and assistant secretaries, the general counsel, and the inspector general.

The DOT works with Congress to formulate transportation legislation. The transportation secretary and the department's legislative counsels work closely with Senate and House committees and subcommittees to address transportation issues. The laws they formulate determine the department's scope and direct its programs.

New York governor Nelson Rockefeller rides a Manhattan subway in 1967 during his campaign to win support for the state's transportation bond issue.

Because Congress approves the federal budget, the department depends on Congress for a large portion of its funding. But unlike many federal agencies, the DOT generates most of its own revenue by collecting highway tolls, gasoline taxes, and other transportation-related tariffs. The department's 1987 budget request, for example, stated that 84 percent of DOT funds would be generated through transportation fees. In this way, the DOT has been able to remain somewhat independent of financial restraints imposed by Congress in any one year.

The Federal-State Relationship

State transportation departments developed after the DOT. In 1967 governors of such states as New York and New Jersey began calling for their own state departments to consolidate and coordinate interstate transportation networks. They organized these departments in much the same way as the federal

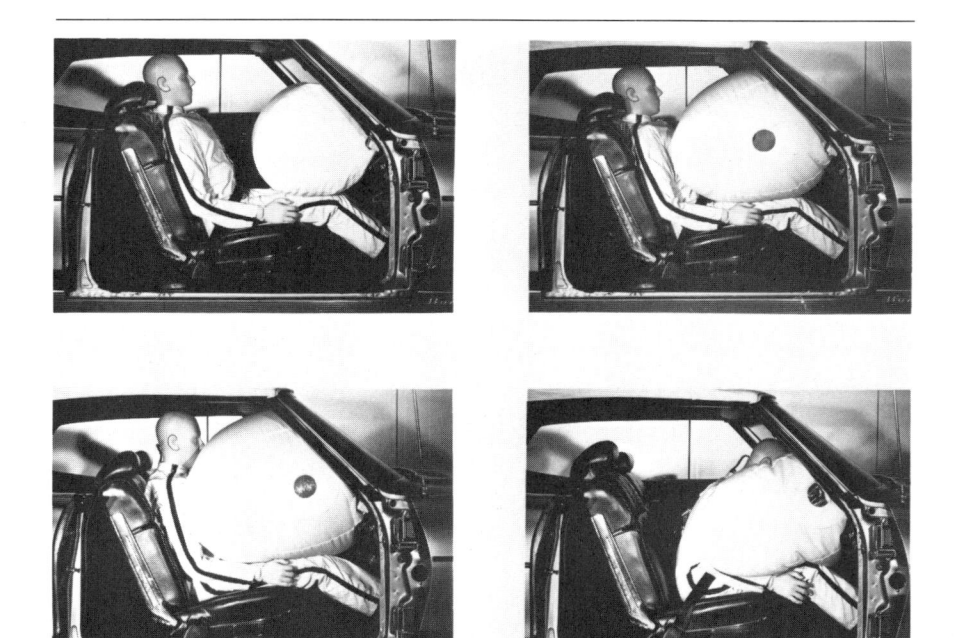

An air bag is tested for efficiency during a simulated car crash. The DOT conducted tests like this one as part of its research for improving safety standards during the late 1960s.

government organized the DOT. State transportation departments are responsible for monitoring various modes of transportation, building and maintaining efficient networks of transportation, and protecting the safety of people traveling within state borders.

The DOT works closely with state transportation departments, helping them promote transportation safety and develop programs. In return, state transportation departments must report their activities, programs, and statistics to the federal government.

Although state transportation departments rely on state legislatures for most of their funding, they also receive some assistance from the DOT. States must comply with DOT regulations to receive certain federal grants. For example, the Boating Safety Financial Assistance grant is available only to states that follow the U.S. Coast Guard's approved boating safety guidelines. Other grants are tied to financial need rather than to compliance with regulations. Highway Planning and Construction grants, for example, help states construct and rehabilitate interstate, primary, and secondary roads and urban streets that could not be built or repaired without federal assistance.

The department also funds programs to educate and train state transportation department employees. For example, Highway Educational grants help train state and local highway department employees in such fields as highway safety and energy conservation.

The Woodrow Wilson Bridge in Maryland is widened to allow for additional two-way traffic. The DOT's Federal Highway Aid program helps fund projects that promote safety and efficiency on the nation's roads.

SIX

Regulating Transportation

Although the DOT has undergone many structural changes since its creation, its primary function has remained the same. It still strives to ensure transportation safety and protect consumer interests. It also helps cities and states cope with their local transportation needs and design plans for future transportation networks and facilities. It performs these diverse tasks by coordinating the efforts of nine operating agencies, each one equipped with its own director, staff, and budget.

The U.S. Coast Guard

The U.S. Coast Guard was established in 1915 and joined the DOT when it was first created in 1966. It protects life and property in and on all navigable waters within U.S. jurisdiction. Using a network of rescue vessels, aircraft, and communications facilities stationed around the nation, the U.S. Coast Guard rescues thousands of people and vessels from danger on the nation's waterways every year.

In addition, the U.S. Coast Guard serves as the nation's primary maritime law enforcement agency. It monitors the compliance of both private and commercial vessels with federal maritime laws. It also cooperates with other federal agencies, such as the Drug Enforcement Administration, to ensure that federal laws are not violated at sea.

Among many other functions, the U.S. Coast Guard also administers and enforces safety standards for both commercial vessels and offshore structures, such as oil rigs, and conducts harbor patrols and waterfront security inspections. It establishes and maintains navigation systems, such as lighthouses, beacons, and radio-navigational signals. It also operates icebreaking vessels to facilitate maritime transportation. In addition, the U.S. Coast Guard works to protect the marine environment and clean up oil and chemical spills.

During wartime, the U.S. Coast Guard becomes part of the U.S. Navy and helps defend the nation on the seas. As commander in chief, the president can mobilize the Coast Guard as a branch of the U.S. armed forces when necessary.

Graduates of the U.S. Merchant Marine Academy toss their hats in celebration. The Merchant Marine consists of the nation's fleet of commercial ships.

The Coast Guard Auxiliary is a volunteer organization that helps the Coast Guard protect the seafaring public. Auxiliary members—most of whom own small boats, aircraft, or radio stations—conduct boating education programs and participate in search and rescue operations.

The Maritime Administration

The Maritime Administration promotes U.S. commercial shipping through a variety of grant and development programs. For example, it provides funds to promote the development and operation of the U.S. Merchant Marine (the nation's fleet of commercial ships) and the Merchant Marine Academy. It also administers federal subsidies to ship operators and builders to support construction and renovation projects.

The Maritime Administration also works to support the business activities of U.S. commercial ships. It conducts programs to develop ports, facilities, and domestic shipping. And it protects merchant ships by offering them war-risk insurance—covering life and property losses attributed to wartime activities—when commercial insurance companies refuse to provide this coverage.

The Saint Lawrence Seaway Development Corporation

The Saint Lawrence Seaway Development Corporation was established to provide safe and efficient transportation for commercial ships traveling on the portion of the Saint Lawrence Seaway that is within the United States. The agency supports itself by charging tolls to vessels using the seaway. It also encourages economic and environmental development in the Great Lakes region by supporting the growth of commercial traffic through the area.

The Federal Highway Administration

The Federal Highway Administration (FHA) works to safeguard people traveling on the nation's highways. It oversees the performance of more than 4 million commercial vehicles and 22,000 hazardous material carriers that operate on national highways, conducting roadside vehicle checks and auditing drivers and safety management procedures at carrier stops.

The FHA administers the Federal Highway Aid program, which grants states financial assistance for highway construction projects and improvements. The program emphasizes funding high-priority projects, such as improving highway design to increase safety, fixing or replacing deficient bridges, and reducing traffic congestion. States often match grants provided by the FHA to establish highway construction and safety programs in accordance with national standards. Other Highway Aid Program activities focus on providing vehicle access to the handicapped and preserving natural beauty along highways. Another FHA project, the Federal Lands Highway Program, provides money to develop and maintain highways, park roads, parkways, and Indian reservation roads.

The National Highway Traffic Safety Administration

The National Highway Traffic Safety Administration (NHTSA) was established in 1970 to reduce the number of deaths, injuries, and economic losses caused

Highway drivers observe the 55 mile-per-hour speed limit during the fuel shortage of the 1970s. The National Highway Traffic Safety Administration makes sure that states enforce the national maximum speed limit.

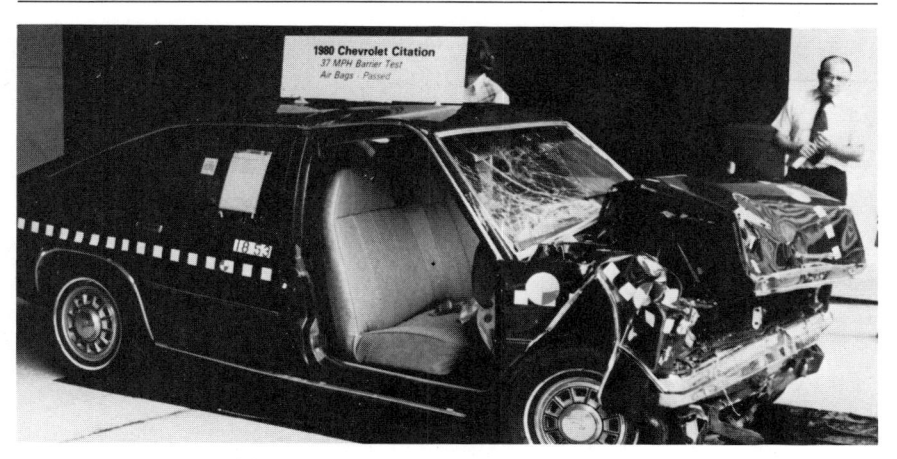

A 1980 Chevrolet Citation as it appeared after a crash test conducted by the DOT's National Highway Traffic Safety Administration. This agency uses crash test results to set automotive safety standards.

by traffic accidents on the nation's highways. It creates programs and enforces regulations that emphasize motor vehicle safety. For example, it promotes the use of seat belts and shoulder harnesses in automobiles and sponsors programs to teach the public about the dangers of drunk or drugged driving. It also maintains a data base of safety information about automobiles, including crash-test results, damage statistics, and consumer complaints about specific car models.

The administration calculates vehicle safety in accidents and studies techniques to avoid vehicle collisions. It monitors states' enforcement of national maximum speed limits set by Congress. It also sets automotive fuel economy standards that manufacturers must meet in building passenger cars. In addition, the NHTSA administers programs and matches funds to help states implement driver, pedestrian, and motor vehicle safety programs.

The Federal Aviation Administration

The Federal Aviation Administration (FAA) issues and enforces air traffic rules and regulations. It sets standards and guidelines for aircraft manufacture, operation, and maintenance. Through its network of airport traffic control towers, the FAA monitors the use of navigable airspace within the United States. It also administers programs that certify pilots and airports.

Public Transportation for the Handicapped

Until the 1970s, physically handicapped Americans had limited access to public transportation. Most of the mass transit systems in operation at that time had not been designed for use by the disabled. As a result, people who relied on wheelchairs, crutches, or other mobility aids found it difficult to use public transportation, which was readily accessible to able-bodied Americans.

The American Coalition of Citizens with Disabilities (ACCD) lobbied for the rights of the handicapped and helped convince Congress to pass the Rehabilitation Act of 1973. Section 504 of this law states that "No otherwise qualified handicapped individual in the United States . . . shall, solely by reason of his handicap, be excluded from participation in, be denied benefits of, or be subjected to discrimination under any program or activity receiving federal financial assistance."

Although few people disputed the need for such legislation, many disagreed about how to implement it. The law's vague wording offered little guidance to the federal agencies that had to enforce its mandate.

In 1979, the Department of Transportation (DOT) attempted to enforce Section 504 by setting standards for mass transit companies in urban areas. These standards called for the installation of wheelchair lifts in all federally funded buses within 10 years, and for the construction of elevators and ramps in key subway stations, such as those near hospitals, within 30 years. The DOT also set stringent accessibility standards for commuter rail systems, airports, highway rest stops, and intercity trains.

According to the Congressional Budget Office (CBO), however, following the DOT's regulations would cost the mass transit industry an estimated $6.8 billion over 30 years. Some critics of the DOT's regulations also questioned whether the number of handicapped people using public transportation would justify the cost of revamping these systems on such a wide scale.

A lobbying group called the American Public Transit Association (APTA) acted to reform the DOT's regulations. The APTA wanted the federal government to permit local mass transit systems to choose the best means of obeying Section 504. It suggested that communities use specially equipped vans and taxis to transport handicapped people to and from their jobs each working day.

The CBO estimated that this service would cost less than $5 billion to implement nationwide and would serve more disabled people than the number that would be served by adapting transit systems according to the DOT's regulations. The ACCD, however, argued that since the vans and taxis would primarily be used to transport handicapped people to and from work, these people would still have limited access to other areas of the community.

In 1981, the U.S. Circuit Court of Appeals in Washington ruled that the DOT's 1979 regulations went beyond what Congress had in mind when it passed Section 504. As a result, the DOT replaced its regulations with a much less stringent set of temporary standards, pending further action by Congress. In January 1983, Congress ordered the DOT to create a new set of permanent regulations. The DOT's revised regulations became effective in May 1986. They allowed local transit systems to choose the mode of transportation that they would adapt for the handicapped, subject to the DOT's approval. They also required the local transit systems to spend 3 percent of their total operating costs on providing such services.

The conflict between the rights of handicapped individuals to use public transportation and the high cost of making this service available to them continues to concern the DOT, Congress, and lobbyists for the handicapped and the mass transit industry. Nonetheless, advocates for the handicapped have made significant gains toward securing equal access for disabled Americans who use public transportation.

A mechanized lift helps a woman in a wheelchair board a city bus. In many metropolitan areas, handicapped riders have access to mass transit vehicles equipped with devices for the disabled.

The FAA maintains a national plan of airport safety requirements and administers programs that fund airport planning and development. Among its goals for the nation's airports are to improve airport security, to meet current and future capacity needs, and to minimize the impact of air traffic on the surrounding environment.

This agency also promotes civil aviation abroad by training foreign nationals, exchanging information with foreign governments, and providing technical representation for the United States at international conferences. In addition, it researches and develops the systems, facilities, and devices needed for safe and efficient air navigation and air traffic control.

Elevated railcars are part of the mass transit system in Washington, D.C. The Urban Mass Transportation Administration funds research to develop transportation networks for America's cities.

The Urban Mass Transportation Administration

The Urban Mass Transportation Administration manages a variety of grant and loan programs that support developments in mass transportation facilities, equipment, and techniques. It promotes the planning and development of surface transportation systems—buses, trolleys, and subways—and assists state and local governments in financing these systems.

The administration funds research and development projects involving such topics as energy-saving buses and rail cars, computerized systems planning, and special transportation for the elderly and handicapped. It also funds university research that explores ways to improve urban mass transportation.

The Federal Railroad Administration

The Federal Railroad Administration (FRA) enforces rail safety laws and develops policies and projects related to railroad finance, planning, and operation. It regulates such matters as service schedules, equipment standards, railroad track maintenance, and transportation of hazardous materials. The FRA aids efforts to rehabilitate passenger service in the northeastern United States, where passenger rails are most prevalent. It also provides federal assistance to national, regional, and local rail services.

The FRA oversees the Transportation Test Center in Pueblo, Colorado. This facility, managed and staffed by the Association of American Railroads, a private organization, tests the soundness of railroad design plans, evaluates the efficiency of existing railroad operations, and examines the impact of railroad transportation systems on the surrounding environment.

Research and Special Programs Administration

Established in 1977, the Research and Special Programs Administration includes six divisions that develop programs and regulations. The Office of Hazardous Materials Transportation develops and issues regulations for transporting hazardous materials by all methods except bulk transport by water. It also gathers and analyzes accident data pertaining to hazardous

Workers construct the Alaska pipeline. The Office of Pipeline Safety sets safety standards for transporting hazardous liquid and gaseous materials through pipelines.

material transport. In addition, the office sponsors programs that inform transportation industry personnel of regulations and train federal and state inspectors to enforce them.

Another division, the Office of Pipeline Safety, establishes and enforces safety standards for transporting hazardous liquid and gaseous materials through pipelines. It sponsors training programs for industry personnel and for federal and state inspectors. It also administers a program that supports state efforts to initiate or broaden intrastate (within a state) pipeline safety programs. One of the division's largest tasks lies in administering the Alaska oil pipeline program.

The Research and Special Programs Administration also includes the Transportation Systems Center, a unit that compiles research and analyses on all existing modes of transportation. Located in Cambridge, Massachusetts, it supports the DOT by developing and maintaining files on national transportation statistics and related information. The center also conducts technical research that provides a basis for development of federal transportation policy.

Other units in the Research and Special Programs Administration include the Office of Emergency Transportation, which develops plans to prepare the department to handle an emergency, such as a natural disaster that might affect transportation; the Office of Aviation Information Management, which collects and distributes information about air carrier operations; and the Office of Program Management and Administration, which provides administrative support services.

Highways crisscross a tree-covered landscape. One of the DOT's ongoing concerns is to promote both beauty and safety on the nation's roads.

SEVEN

Transportation and the Future

The DOT has adopted a broad range of duties since it was created in 1966. Perhaps most significantly, the DOT has raised public awareness of transportation safety. It has encouraged seat belt use, cautioned against drunk or drugged driving, and designed safe boating and air traffic regulations. In other areas, it has funded construction for thousands of miles of highway, improved the beauty and safety of the nation's roads, and recalled defective cars. It has salvaged deteriorating railroads and addressed numerous problems concerning urban mass transportation.

Despite the DOT's accomplishments, many problems still plague America's transportation systems. For example, the nation still depends on foreign oil to fuel its motor vehicles. In the 1970s, the department set a uniform maximum speed limit of 55 miles per hour and advocated the use of commuter carpools to conserve fuel and thereby reduce America's dependence on foreign oil. When the world's oil prices and supplies stabilized in the late 1980s, the public demanded higher speed limits, and Congress passed legislation permitting traffic to travel at 65 miles per hour on some of the country's highways. Nevertheless, the DOT continues to explore alternative ways to fuel motor vehicles in case the nation faces another oil shortage in the future.

Economic problems will continue to concern the DOT. Developing and

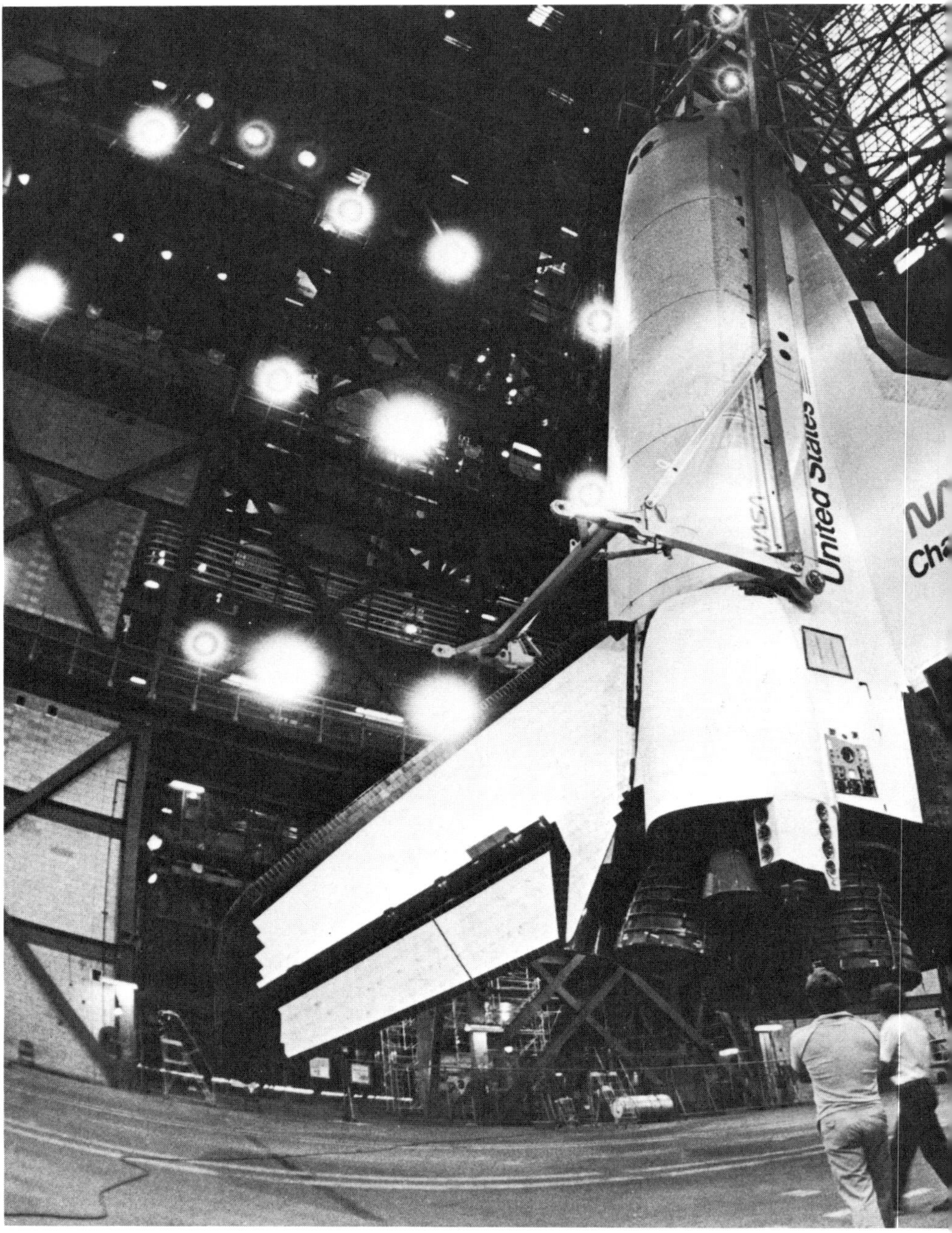
NASA
United States

The space shuttle Challenger, prior to its fatal 1986 flight. Advances in transportation, perhaps including space travel, will challenge the DOT in the future.

A sign in front of a Washington, D.C., gas station warns customers that gas will be sold by appointment only. To conserve fuel during the 1970s, the DOT advocated gas rationing.

improving transportation systems requires billions of dollars in funding. But as Congress tries to trim the huge federal deficit, the DOT will compete with other government agencies for available funds. Anticipating such problems, the DOT has tried to cut internal costs; its 1987 budget request was nearly $8 billion less than its 1985 appropriation.

Advances in transportation will also challenge the department. New forms of transportation are sure to replace older methods, just as railroads replaced canal boats in the 19th century. These new transportation systems will create new problems. Space travel, for example, could become relatively common in the 21st century. The department may be expected to regulate such travel and to coordinate its efforts with other nations.

In addition, technological advances will affect the DOT's future. Some analysts predict that improvements in telecommunications such as videotext (communication technology that allows people to see an image as well as hear a voice over telephone lines)—will reduce the need for travel, particularly business travel.

Finally, American attitudes and public opinion will certainly play a role in deciding the course of the department's future. The public determines the popularity of different forms of transportation. It also makes clear what types of regulations are necessary and when they should be implemented. In 1986 a DOT survey revealed that most Americans dislike excessive regulation and prefer innovative programs, such as fuel-efficient automobiles, to mandatory solutions, such as gas rationing. The department's future programs will need to respond to these attitudes.

The DOT has assumed hundreds of different jobs while regulating the quality and growth of national transportation. It researches the viability of future transportation methods, while examining the continued efficiency of existing systems. The department also attends to specific goals of the president and Congress, while heeding public opinion. It sets safety and environmental standards, while debating the merits of greater speed and convenience in transportation systems. These factors will help shape the DOT's future efforts and influence its policies and programs. Technological innovations, economic demands, and public preferences will determine how the nation uses its transportation systems. These systems will continue to develop as they always have—in response to the nation's changing needs.

The Department of Transportation Organization

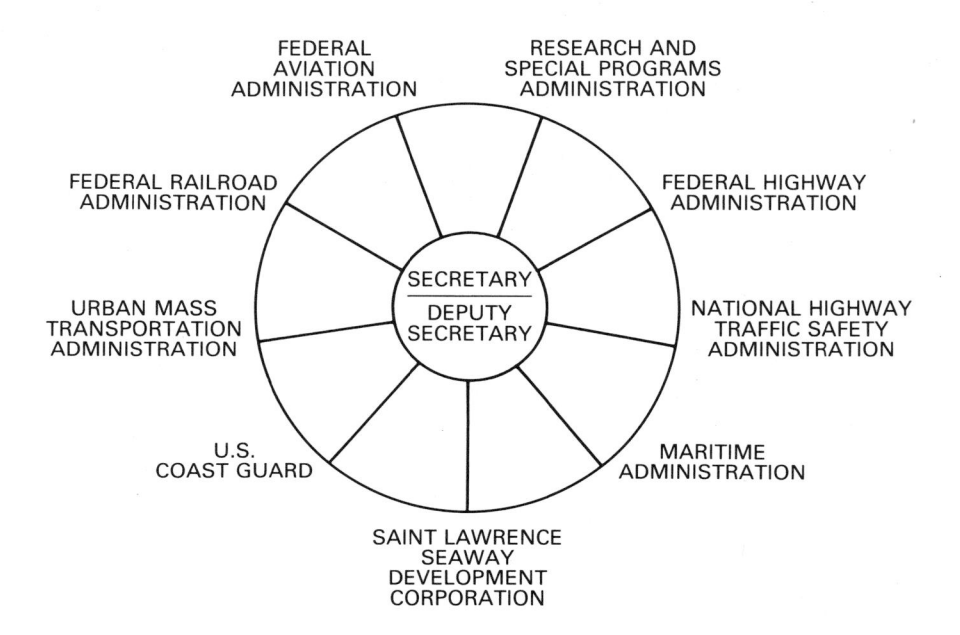

- FEDERAL AVIATION ADMINISTRATION
- RESEARCH AND SPECIAL PROGRAMS ADMINISTRATION
- FEDERAL RAILROAD ADMINISTRATION
- FEDERAL HIGHWAY ADMINISTRATION
- URBAN MASS TRANSPORTATION ADMINISTRATION
- NATIONAL HIGHWAY TRAFFIC SAFETY ADMINISTRATION
- U.S. COAST GUARD
- MARITIME ADMINISTRATION
- SAINT LAWRENCE SEAWAY DEVELOPMENT CORPORATION

SECRETARY
DEPUTY SECRETARY

GLOSSARY

Amtrak The federally supported National Railroad Passenger Corporation; created by the government in 1970 by combining financially troubled passenger railroads to establish a national network.

Canal An artificial waterway built by digging a trench between two bodies of water.

Common carrier A transportation system designed to carry passengers.

Conrail The Consolidated Rail Corporation; created by the government in 1973 to restructure the failing northeastern rail freight system.

Corduroy road A road made of logs or wood planks laid side by side; developed in the 1770s.

Deregulation The reduction or removal of federal restrictions governing the operation of a company or industry; applied to the airline industry in 1978 and to the trucking and rail industries in 1980.

Intermodal transportation The use of two or more transportation methods.

Interstate Refers to transportation between two or more states.

Intrastate Refers to transportation within the borders of a single state.

Land grant A plot of land granted to a state by the federal government to help fund construction of roads or railroads.

Macadam road A road surfaced with crushed rock; named for Scottish inventor Loudon McAdam.

Mass transit The system of urban public transportation that includes subways, buses, and trains.

Monopoly An unfair advantage, such as that experienced by a company facing little or no competition and exercising control of its market.

Regulate The function of state and federal agencies to set standards and requirements for businesses and industries.

Turnpike A state-maintained toll road.

SELECTED REFERENCES

Dolan, J. R. *The Yankee Peddlers of Early America*. New York: Potter, 1964.

Drago, Harry S. *Canal Days in America*. New York: Bramhall House, 1972.

Fischler, Stanley I. *Moving Millions*. New York: Harper & Row, 1979.

Hilton, Suzanne. *Faster Than a Horse—Moving West with Engine Power*. Philadelphia: The Westminister Press, 1983.

Lesstrang, Jacques. *Seaway*. Vancouver: Evergreen Press Ltd., 1976.

National Transportation Policy Study Commission. *National Transportation Policies through the Year 2000*. Washington, D.C.: U. S. Government Printing Office, 1979.

Scalberg, Carl. *Conquest of the Skies*. Boston: Little, Brown, 1979.

Sobel, Robert. *The Fallen Colossus*. New York: Weybright and Talley, 1977.

U.S. Department of Transportation. *Transportation and the Future*. Washington, D.C.: U. S. Government Printing Office, 1979.

INDEX

Adams, Brock, 52, 54
Administration, Office of, 64
Airline Deregulation Act of 1978, 54
Air Safety Board, 34, 36
Air traffic controllers, 63
Air travel, 34, 36, 39, 40, 45, 60, 61
Alaska, 81
Alaska Railroad, 42, 43
Albany, New York, 23
American Coalition of Citizens with Disabilities (ACCD), 76
American Public Transit Association (APTA), 76
Amtrak, 51, 52, 60, 61
Army Signal Corps, 34
Association of American Railroads, 79
Atlanta, Georgia, 63
Atlantic Ocean, 34
Automobiles, 33, 39, 40, 41, 60, 75
Aviation Information Management, Office of, 81

Baltimore and Ohio Railroad, 26, 27
Best Friend of Charleston, The, 27
Boating Safety Financial Assistance grant, 69
Boston, Massachusetts, 19
Boston Post Road, 19
Boyd, Alan S., 47, 48, 50
Brinegar, Claude, 52
Budget and Programs, Office of, 64
Buffalo, New York, 23
Bureau of Motor Carrier Safety, 43
Bureau of Public Roads, 42, 43
Bureau of Railroad Safety, 43
Buses, 16, 39, 49, 60, 66, 76, 79

Cambridge, Massachusetts, 81
Canals, 22, 23, 26, 27, 29–31, 86
Capehart, Homer, 37
Carter, Jimmy, 52
Charleston, South Carolina, 27
Chicago, Illinois, 63
Civil Aeronautics Act of 1938, 34
Civil Aeronautics Authority, 34, 36
Civil Aeronautics Board (CAB), 36, 42, 47, 54, 59
Civil Rights, Office of, 65
Clinton, DeWitt, 23
Coast Guard, U.S., 16, 42, 43, 47, 66, 69, 71–73
Coast Guard Auxiliary, 73
Commerce, Department of, 37, 43, 45
Commercial Space Transportation, Office of, 65
Commission on Organization of the Executive Branch of Government, 37
Congress, U.S., 20–22, 32–34, 36, 42, 43, 45, 51, 52, 54, 59–61, 64, 66, 68, 76, 77, 83, 86, 87
Congressional Budget Office (CBO), 76
Conrail, 52, 59–61
Consolidated Rail Corporation, 52. *See also* Conrail
Contract Appeals Board, 65
Cooper, Peter, 27
Corduroy roads, 20
Cumberland, Maryland, 20
Cumberland Road, 20

Deregulation, 54, 60, 61
Dole, Elizabeth H., 57, 59
Drug Enforcement Administration, 72

Emergency Transportation, Office of, 81
Erie Canal, 23

Federal Aid Road Act, 33
Federal Aviation Administration (FAA), 16, 43, 48, 66, 75, 78
Federal Aviation Agency, 42, 55
Federal Highway Administration (FHA), 16, 43, 49, 66, 73, 74
Federal Highway Aid, 74
Federal Labor Relations Authority, 56
Federal Lands Highway Program, 74
Federal Railroad Administration (FRA), 16, 43, 48, 66, 79
Fitch, John, 21
Ford, Henry, 33
Fort Worth, Texas, 63

General Counsel, Office of the, 63
Governmental Affairs, Office of, 64
Great Lakes, 73
Great Lakes Pilotage Administration, 42

Handicapped Americans, 76, 77
Hazardous Materials Transportation, Office of, 79
High-Speed Ground Transportation, Office of, 43
Highway Beautification Act, 49
Highway Educational grants, 69

Highway Planning and Construction grant, 69
Highway Safety Act, 47
Hoover, Herbert, 37
House of Representatives, U.S., 43, 59, 66
Hudson River, 19, 23

Indiana, 37
Indians, American, 19, 21
Inspector General, Office of the, 54, 63
Interstate Commerce Act, 32
Interstate Commerce Commission (ICC), 32, 34, 42, 48, 54
"Iron horse." *See* railroads

Jackson, Andrew, 27
Johnson, Lyndon, 41, 42, 45, 47, 50

Kansas City, Missouri, 63
Kitty Hawk, 32

Lake Erie, 23, 66
Lancaster, Pennsylvania, 20
Lewis, Drew, 56, 57
Lindbergh, Charles, 34

McAdam, Loudon, 20
Macadamized roads, 20
Maritime Administration, 16, 42, 45, 66, 73
Massachusetts, 50
Materials Transportation Bureau, 54
Merchant Marine, U.S., 73
Merchant Marine Academy, 73
Minority Business Resource Center, 65
Mississippi, 21
Mississippi River, 22
Model T, 33
Montreal, Canada, 66
Motor Carrier Act of 1980, 54

Nader, Ralph, 41
Natchez Trace, 21
National Highway Safety Advisory Committee, 47
National Highway Safety Bureau, 43
National Highway Traffic Safety Administration (NHTSA), 16, 66, 74, 75
National Pike, 20, 21
National Railroad Passenger Corporation, 51. *See also* Amtrak
National Traffic and Motor Vehicle Safety Act, 47
National Transportation Safety Board (NTSB), 45
Navy, U.S., 72
Nebraska, 37
New Jersey, 69
New Orleans, Louisiana, 21
New York, 69
New York City, New York, 19, 23, 34, 48
New York Stock Exchange, 59
Nixon, Richard, 50
Norfolk Southern Corporation, 59

Ohio River, 22

Pennsylvania, 23
Philadelphia, Pennsylvania, 20, 23, 34, 63
Pipelines, 17, 45, 54, 81
Pipeline Safety, Office of, 81
Pittsburgh, Pennsylvania, 23
Policy and International Affairs, Office of, 64
Post Office Department, U.S., 34
Professional Air Traffic Controllers Organization (PATCO), 55–57
Program Management and Administration, Office of, 81

Public Affairs, Office of, 64
Public Law 89-670, 43
Pueblo, Colorado, 79

Rail Passenger Service Act of 1970, 51
Railroad Revitalization and Regulatory Reform Act of 1976, 52
Railroads, 26–33, 36, 39, 40, 45, 48, 51, 52, 54, 59–61, 66, 79, 83, 86
Reagan, Ronald, 56, 57, 59, 61
Regional Rail Reorganization Act, 52
Rehabilitation Act of 1973, 76
Relay, Maryland, 27
Research and Special Programs Administration, 16, 54, 66, 79, 81

Saint Lawrence River, 66
Saint Lawrence Seaway, 73
Saint Lawrence Seaway Development Corporation, 16, 42, 43, 66, 73
San Francisco, California, 34, 63
Seat belts, 57, 83
Secretary, Office of the, 50, 52, 54, 63
Senate, U.S., 43, 59, 66
Space travel, 86
Speed limit, 16, 57, 75
Staggers Rail Act of 1980, 54, 60
Steamboats, 21, 22
Stefan, Karl, 37
Subways, 16, 49, 66, 76, 79

Taxis, 39
Telecommunications, 87
Tice Law, 33
Toll roads, 20
Tom Thumb, the, 27
Transportation Programs Bureau, 54

Transportation safety, 16, 41, 43, 47, 51, 71, 78
Transportation Systems Center, 54, 81
Transportation Test Center, 79
Treasury, Department of, 43
Trevithick, Richard, 26
Trolleys, 16, 49, 66, 79
Trucking, 54
Turnpikes, 20

Under Secretary of Commerce for Transportation, Office of the, 42
Unsafe at Any Speed (Nader), 41

Urban Mass Transportation Administration, 16, 49, 66, 79
U.S. Circuit Court of Appeals, 76

Van Buren, Martin, 27
Vandalia, 21
Videotext, 87
Volpe, John A., 50–52

Washington, D.C., 34, 63, 76
World War II, 39
Wright Brothers, 32

Wallace Charles Stefany is a communications consultant based in Oakton, Virginia. Formerly the director of public affairs for the Department of Transportation and a member of the Civil Aeronautics Board, he has also served as a reporter and a columnist. He holds an A.B. from Muhlenberg College.

Arthur M. Schlesinger, jr., served in the White House as special assistant to Presidents Kennedy and Johnson. He is the author of numerous acclaimed works in American history and has twice been awarded the Pulitzer Prize. He taught history at Harvard College for many years and is currently Albert Schweitzer Professor of the Humanities at the City College of New York.

PICTURE CREDITS:

Courtesy of Amtrak: cover (bottom right); AP/Wide World Photos: pp. 37, 42, 44, 46, 55, 57, 62, 67, 80, 84–85; courtesy of the Department of Transportation: cover (top), pp. 2, 16, 17, 48, 49, 50–51, 53, 58, 70, 82; Library of Congress: pp. 14, 20–21, 23, 26, 28–29, 30, 31, 32, 33, 35, 41; Paul Myatt: p. 78; National Archives: pp. 18, 22, 24–25, 38, 40; The Port of Seattle: p. 65; Phil Portlock: p. 77; Donald A. Pyle: p. 43; UPI/Bettmann Newsphotos: pp. 36, 56, 63, 74; courtesy of the U.S. Coast Guard: cover (bottom left); U.S. Merchant Marine Academy: p. 72; *Washington Star* collection: p. 86.

HE
206.3
.S73
1988

14.95

HE
206.3
.S73

1988